Squishy Circuits

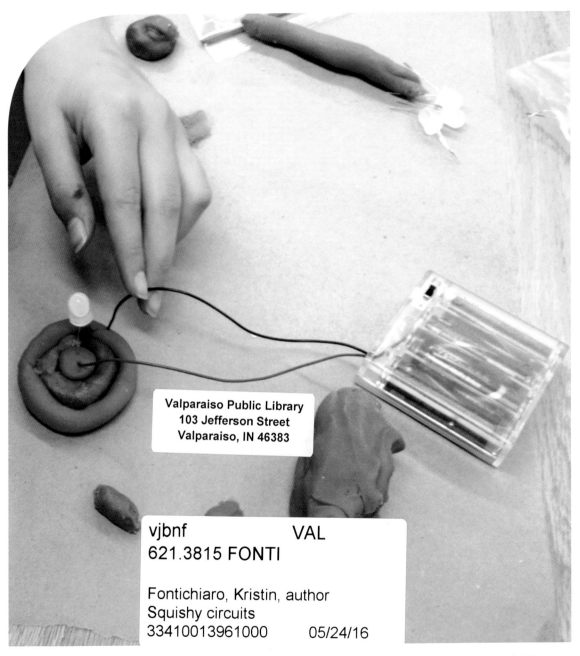

CHERRY LAKE PUBLISHING • ANN ARBOR, MICHIGAN   **by Kristin Fontichiaro and AnnMarie P. Thomas**

A Note to Adults: Please review the instructions for the activities in this book before allowing children to do them. Be sure to help them with any activities you do not think they can safely complete on their own.

A Note to Kids: Be sure to ask an adult for help with these activities when you need it. Always put your safety first!

Published in the United States of America by Cherry Lake Publishing
Ann Arbor, Michigan
www.cherrylakepublishing.com

Series editor: Kristin Fontichiaro

Photo Credits: Cover and pages 1, 7, 11, 12, 14, 20, 22, 24, 25, and 26, courtesy of Michigan Makers; page 4, Jacob Davies/www.flickr.com/ CC BY-SA 2.0; page 5, aplumb/www.flickr.com/CC BY-SA 2.0; pages 9, 18, 21, and 29, courtesy of AnnMarie Thomas; page 16, 33078680@N08/ www.flickr.com/CC BY-SA 2.0; page 23, oskay/www.flickr.com/CC BY 2.0.

Library of Congress Cataloging-in-Publication Data
Fontichiaro, Kristin, author.
  Squishy circuits / by Kristin Fontichiaro and AnnMarie P. Thomas.
    pages cm. — (Makers as innovators)
  Summary: "Learn how to create electronic circuits using modeling dough."—Provided by publisher.
  Audience: Grades 4 to 6.
  Includes bibliographical references and index.
  ISBN 978-1-63137-775-4 (lib. bdg.) — ISBN 978-1-63137-795-2 (pbk.) — ISBN 978-1-63137-835-5 (e-book) — ISBN 978-1-63137-815-7 (pdf)
  1. Electronic circuit design—Technique—Juvenile literature. 2. Polymer clay craft—Juvenile literature. 3. Modeling—Juvenile literature. 4. Play-Doh (Toy)—Juvenile literature. [1. Clay modeling.] I. Thomas, AnnMarie P., author. II. Title.
  TK7870.F54 2014
  621.3815—dc23   2014001369

Cherry Lake Publishing would like to acknowledge the work of The Partnership for 21st Century Skills. Please visit www.p21.org for more information.

Printed in the United States of America
Corporate Graphics Inc.
July 2014

Contents

Chapter 1

Inventing Squishy Circuits

Electrical **circuits** are all around us. They are in radios, stoplights, computers, and countless other things we encounter every day.

Some people teach classes about building electrical circuits. One of those people is the coauthor of this book, AnnMarie Thomas. She is a college engineering professor, and she works with students on design projects.

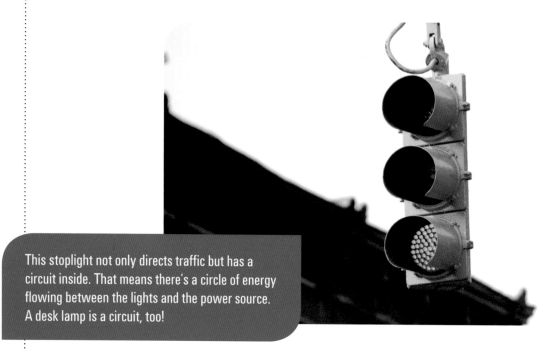

This stoplight not only directs traffic but has a circuit inside. That means there's a circle of energy flowing between the lights and the power source. A desk lamp is a circuit, too!

AnnMarie Thomas (right) introduces Squishy Circuits at an outdoor festival for makers.

AnnMarie wanted to share her enthusiasm for building circuits with her preschool-age daughter. However, she also wanted her daughter to be safe. Even though electricity is all around us, it can be dangerous if we are not careful. In addition, connecting electrical wires by **soldering** usually requires the use of high-temperature tools. AnnMarie wanted to come up with a safer way of connecting circuits.

AnnMarie and one of her students, Sam, learned that some teachers had used modeling dough in experiments to see if it conducts electricity. They also found that researchers at the Massachusetts Institute of Technology (MIT) and other places had used dough in some of their circuit-building projects. However, AnnMarie and Sam didn't find anyone who had used dough to actually build circuits that had lights, sound, or movement. Sam and AnnMarie thought that they could use dough to make safe circuits that were also cool sculptures.

Are You a Maker?

No matter what kinds of tools and materials you use or what projects you like to work on, the act of creating something makes you a **maker**. If you stitch, saw, solder, or staple, you're a maker. If you tinker, putter, play, plan, program, throw it out, and start again, you're a maker. If you use wood, paper, plastic, fabric, wire, junk, or computers, you're a maker. If you share what you know and can't wait to learn what you don't, you're a maker. If seeing problems inspires you to figure out solutions, you're a maker.

A makerspace is a place where makers come together to share ideas, tools, and skills. Sometimes, these spaces are called by other names, such as hackerspaces, guilds, clubs, or studios.

All summer, Sam and AnnMarie tried out dough recipes in their toy design class. They knew they would need different types of dough. One would need to allow electricity to flow through it. The other would need to prevent electricity from moving through it.

Sam and AnnMarie called their project "Squishy Circuits" and invited middle school students to play with their dough. The middle school students loved tinkering with the dough and helping to improve the

Middle school students tried early versions of Squishy Circuits and gave valuable feedback.

Squishy Circuits project. AnnMarie and Sam started working with other professors and students at their school. They talked to teachers, engineers, chemists, and other people who had ideas about things that could be done with the circuits.

With help from others at their university, AnnMarie and Sam came up with a circuit-building system that was easy, safe, and fun. Throughout the United States and around the world, people started using Squishy Circuits. In science museums, Maker Faires, maker clubs, and schools, people started sculpting circuits out of modeling dough.

Would you like to make your own Squishy Circuits? It all starts with a trip to the hobby shop and the grocery store.

Chapter 2

Gathering Supplies

Most circuits consist of wires and hard circuit boards, but you can build circuits with other materials. With Squishy Circuits, the wires and circuit boards are replaced with two types of modeling dough.

You will need some simple supplies to make your first Squishy Circuits. From the hobby or electronics shop, you will need:

Attaching a Y-shaped metal piece—called a terminal—to the end of a battery pack wire will help electricity spread more efficiently to your circuit.

- A battery pack that can hold four AA batteries and has a built-in switch. Ask for an adult's help in soldering the wires from the battery pack to **terminals** (metal Y-shaped pieces). You can find directions for adding terminals

Recipe for Conductive Dough

Ingredients

1 cup tap water

1 cup flour for dough

½ cup flour for kneading

¼ cup salt

3 tablespoons cream of tartar (or 9 tablespoons lemon juice)

1 tablespoon vegetable oil

Food coloring (optional)

Procedure:

- Mix the water, 1 cup flour, salt, cream of tartar, vegetable oil, and food coloring in a medium pot. (You can also add the food coloring after cooking if you want to make many colors of dough in a single batch.)
- Cook the mixture over medium heat, stirring continuously. The mixture will begin to boil and start to get chunky.
- Keep stirring the mixture until it forms a ball in the center of the pot and begins to look shiny.
- Once a ball forms, place the ball on a lightly floured surface. It will be very hot, so flatten it with a spoon and let it cool for a few minutes before touching it with your hands.
- Slowly knead the dough by rolling it on the floured surface, pressing it with the heel of your hand, folding it in half, and repeating. Sprinkle some of the remaining flour into it if it starts to get sticky.
- If you didn't add food coloring earlier, divide your dough into small pieces about the size of a Ping-Pong ball. Press your finger into each ball to make a little bowl.

Recipe for Conductive Dough (Continued)

Squirt about four drops of food coloring into each bowl. Knead the color into each ball until it is even. Wash off any food coloring that gets on your hands.

- Store your dough in an airtight container or plastic bag. It will last for about two weeks.

at *http://courseweb.stthomas.edu/apthomas/ SquishyCircuits/leads.htm*. The terminals provide more surface area to help the electricity move from the wire to the dough.

- Four AA batteries for the battery pack.
- A light-emitting diode (LED) bulb. We like the jumbo 10-millimeter one for bright light!

Recipe for Insulating Dough

Ingredients

1 cup flour for dough

½ cup sugar

3 tablespoons vegetable oil

½ cup distilled water (you can use regular tap water, but the dough's ability to resist electricity will be lower)

½ cup flour for kneading

Procedure:

- In a pot or large bowl, mix together 1 cup flour, sugar, and oil.
- Add about 1 tablespoon of water. Stir.
- Keep adding 1 tablespoon of water at a time until most of the water has been absorbed by the mixture.
- When the dough is mostly dry and crumbly (as shown in the photo below), scoop it out onto a floured surface. Knead it into a lump.
- Add 1 tablespoon of water at a time until the mixture becomes sticky and doughlike.
- Knead the remaining ½ cup flour into the dough until it feels solid but no longer sticky.

From the grocery store, you will need:

- Flour
- Salt
- Sugar
- Cream of tartar (or lemon juice)
- Vegetable oil
- Food coloring (any color)
- Distilled water
- Tap water

We'll start our circuit building in the kitchen. Find an adult who can help you with the stove or a hot plate.

We need to make two kinds of dough. The first kind will be **conductive** dough. This is a dough that will allow an electrical charge to flow through it. Materials that conduct electricity are known as conductors. Just like a train conductor helps the train get where it is going, conductive materials help energy move along. The most common electrical conductors are metal and water.

You will also make **insulating** dough. It contains only small amounts of conductive ingredients, so only a little electricity can flow through it.

Chapter 3

Building a Circuit

Knowing how electricity works can help you build a successful Squishy Circuit. In this chapter, you'll learn how to make a basic Squishy Circuit and how to troubleshoot a nonworking circuit like this one.

I f you think the word *circuit* sounds like *circle*, you're right. A circuit is like a circle of energy. Energy travels from an energy source (such as a wall outlet or a battery) through something that needs power (such as a lightbulb, a television, or a refrigera-tor) and back again. The energy travels over and over and over again in a circular pattern. It keeps moving in the same direction until you break the circuit by disconnecting the **components** or turning off the power.

Conductive materials help the energy travel. Remember the colored dough you made in Chapter 2? It had salt and water in it. These substances are what make the dough conductive.

Some materials don't help energy travel. If an energy flow meets these materials, the energy won't travel through them. It will try to move around them. These materials are known as insulators. Styrofoam and cardboard are two good examples of insulators. The uncolored dough you made in Chapter 2 doesn't have the right mix of ingredients to conduct energy, so it works as an insulator.

Let's take a look at a beginning Squishy Circuit. Gather the supplies discussed in Chapter 2. Next, take a look at your AA batteries. Have you ever noticed that the two ends of a AA battery are different? One end has a bump sticking out of it. The other end is almost flat.

The positive and negative ends of batteries are clearly labeled with + and − signs.

Now take a look at the labels on the ends of the battery. Do you see how the bump is labeled with a plus sign (+)? That means it's the positive end of the battery. See how the flat end is labeled with a minus sign (−)? That's the negative end. Both the shape and the labels will help you load your battery pack correctly. Inside the pack are metal and wire that connect the batteries together. If you have a see-through battery pack, you'll even see how the red wire connects to the positive end of the first battery and the black wire connects to the negative end of the last battery.

LED bulbs have positive and negative ends, too. If you look closely at your LED bulb, you'll see two small wires sticking out of it like legs. These "legs" are

Many Kinds of Conductors, Many Kinds of Circuits

You can make circuits out of lots of different materials. Most of the time, we think of electricity as flowing through wires. With Squishy Circuits, conductive dough is used in place of these wires.

Electricity can travel through other conductors, too. Does anyone in your family have a hair dryer? Take a look at the warning label on it. Why does it warn you not to use it near the bathtub? Because water is a conductor! Water with electrical current flowing through it can be extremely dangerous.

Some threads are woven with very fine electrical wire, making it possible for you to add circuits to your clothing. These materials are known as e-textiles. Scientists and inventors are working on other ways to make circuits useful to people. Imagine a pair of jeans that could measure the number of steps you take each day!

Sometimes, wires can take up a lot of space in circuits. Makers often look for less bulky conductors. Circuit boards are pieces of metal that have circuit paths etched into them. These conductors are less bulky than wires. So is Bare Conductive paint (*www.bareconductive.com*),

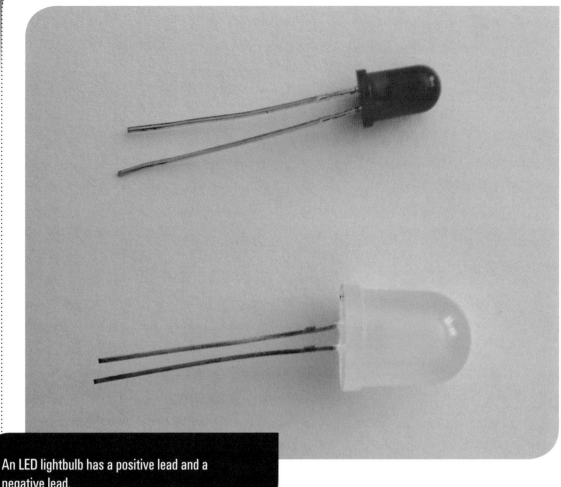

An LED lightbulb has a positive lead and a negative lead.

called **leads**. One is slightly longer than the other. The longer end is the positive end. Not all components have positive and negative ends, though!

It's tempting just to touch the leads of the LED directly to the wires coming out of the battery pack. However, that would send too much energy through the bulb and damage it. We need to build a circuit that conducts electricity without burning out the bulb.

First, we need a piece of conductive dough. Try a piece about the size of a cherry. Stick the positive end of your battery pack (the red wire) and the long positive lead of your LED into one piece of dough. Get a second piece of conductive dough. Stick the short negative lead of the LED and the black negative wire from the battery pack into the second piece. Flip the switch on your battery pack. Your LED should light up. Congratulations! You just made your first Squishy Circuit!

Now try touching the two pieces of dough together. Why did the light turn off? Separate the dough pieces. Why did it come back on? Electricity likes to find the most direct path to travel on. When you connected the two pieces of dough, you made a shorter path. The electricity just traveled through the dough and back to the battery pack. This prevented it from reaching your LED.

To keep your circuit working, you could just try really hard to hold the two pieces of dough apart. Your arms might get tired, though! What if you stuck something that didn't conduct electricity between the two dough pieces? That would force the electricity to flow up through the LED bulb. Try inserting a small piece of insulating dough between the two conductive dough pieces. Your LED should shine brightly again!

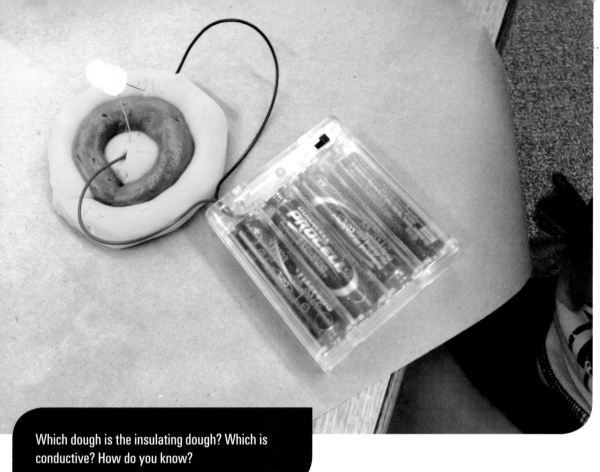

Which dough is the insulating dough? Which is conductive? How do you know?

Try inserting other insulators, too, such as a piece of Styrofoam or cardboard.

The Squishy Circuit in the picture above looks like a bull's-eye. It was made with both conductive and insulating dough. The shape of the dough tricks your eye. In this circuit, both the insulating dough and the conductive dough have been dyed with food coloring. Can you figure out the electricity's path? Which dough is conductive? Which is insulating? How did you figure it out?

If you wanted to add more lights to the circuit, how would you do it? You would need to know about **series circuits** and **parallel circuits**. Keep reading!

Chapter 4

Series and Parallel Circuits

I t's easy to make a simple circuit with just one light-bulb. But once you've mastered that, it's fun to think about circuits with more parts. What if you wanted to have multiple LED bulbs?

How many LED bulbs can you put in a single circuit? It depends, among other things, on the kinds of bulbs, the amount of conductive and insulating dough, and the amount of battery power.

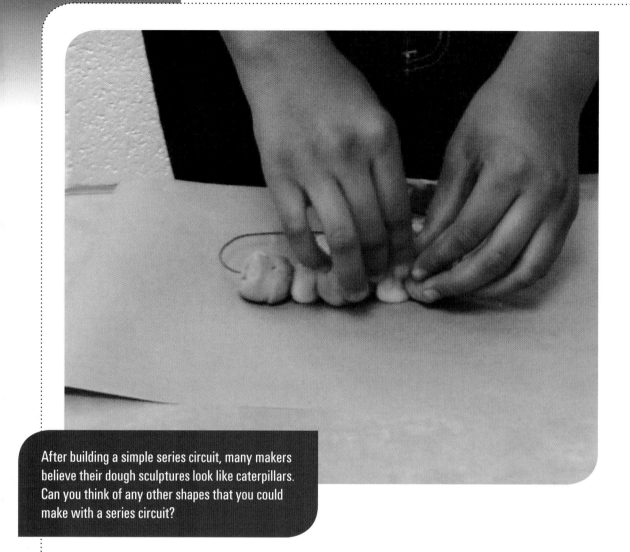

After building a simple series circuit, many makers believe their dough sculptures look like caterpillars. Can you think of any other shapes that you could make with a series circuit?

One way to do this is by making a series circuit. When you read books in a series, you start with Book 1, then read Book 2, and so on. In a series circuit, the electricity flows from the battery to the first bulb, then to a second bulb, and then to any others, and finally back to the battery. In this case,

Resistors

Once you have mastered Squishy Circuits, you can move on to making other kinds of circuits. As you do, you will learn more about the amount of energy that power sources provide and the amount of energy that different components need. If a component gets too much energy, it can overheat or burn. This is what people mean when they say that they "fried" an electronic component.

What do electrical engineers do when a power source delivers more energy than a component needs? They use resistors. Resistors are special components that restrict the amount of electricity that can flow through. They're placed between the energy source and the component in a circuit. Resistors come in different sizes to restrict different amounts of energy. By limiting the amount of energy that flows through them, resistors hold back extra electricity. This protects your component from getting fried. As you become a more experienced electrical engineer, you'll learn the information you need to know about which resistors you should put into your circuit.

When we make Squishy Circuits, the conductive dough has a small amount of resistance built in. This allows us to skip adding resistors to our circuit.

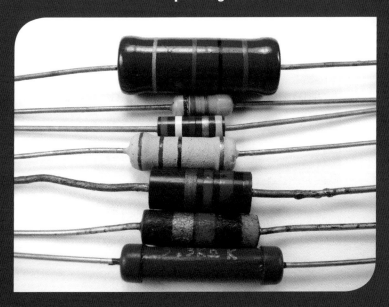

Chapter 5

Challenge Yourself!

Once you have your LED circuits working, you may want to explore adding sound and movement to your circuits. To do this, you will need motors and buzzers.

Choose a motor that requires only a small amount of energy to make it spin. The Squishy Circuits Web site

Do you see the blue insulating dough just peeking through the pink conductive dough? The insulating dough is keeping the leads separate so the energy will flow properly through the circuit.

has a list of motors that work well for this project. We recommend adding terminals to your motor like you did with the battery pack's wires.

To start using a motor, add conductive dough to the leads of your battery pack, just like you did for your first LED circuit in Chapter 3. Now plug one of the motor's terminals into the dough attached to the positive battery pack lead. Connect the other terminal to the dough attached to the negative battery pack lead. Unlike LED bulbs, which have a positive and negative lead, either lead of a motor can connect to the positive lead of a battery pack. Turn your battery pack on and see your motor spin! Now try switching which motor leads are attached to the positive and negative leads of the battery pack. Your motor will start turning in the opposite direction!

A Squishy Circuits Challenge!

Can you sculpt an animal with LED eyes and a spinning tail? Imagine what the circuit would look like before you build it. You could even sketch it out on paper first. Would you use a series circuit? A parallel circuit? Both? Where would you need insulating dough? Where would you need conductive dough?

Another fun thing to do with Squishy Circuits is build musical instruments using a battery pack, conductive dough, and a buzzer. The Squishy Circuits Web site has a list of recommended buzzers. Buzzers have a positive wire and a negative wire. Typically, the positive wire is red, and the negative wire is black. Plug the red wire into the dough that is attached to the battery pack's positive lead. Plug the black wire into the dough that is attached to the battery pack's negative lead. The buzzer should begin buzzing when you turn the battery pack on! If you touch the two lumps of conductive dough together, you will cause the buzzer to either stop buzzing or buzz more quietly, depending on the type of buzzer. Try different buzzers and see if you can make a buzzer orchestra!

Now that you know the basics of Squishy Circuits, you're ready to tackle more complicated projects. Maybe you want your LEDs to flash on and off. Maybe you would like your buzzers to play multiple notes. For that, you'll need to add a small computer, such as an Arduino, to your

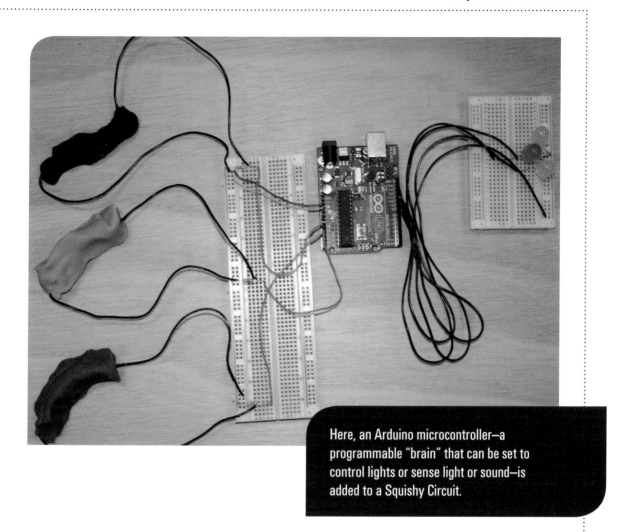

Here, an Arduino microcontroller—a programmable "brain" that can be set to control lights or sense light or sound—is added to a Squishy Circuit.

circuit. Check the Squishy Circuits Web site for directions.

There are an unlimited number of Squishy Circuits you can build. Be creative and see what you can make!

Glossary

circuits (SIR-kits) complete paths for an electrical current

components (kuhm-POH-nuhnts) parts of a larger whole, especially a machine or a system

conductive (kuhn-DUK-tiv) able to allow electricity to pass through

insulating (IN-suh-lay-ting) preventing electricity from passing through

leads (LEEDS) "legs" or wires that help electricity flow more effectively through a component

maker (MAY-kur) someone who invents or creates something

parallel circuits (PAR-uh-lel SIR-kits) circuits in which energy flows through two or more paths at once

series circuits (SEER-eez SIR-kits) circuits in which energy flows from one component to the next, in order

soldering (SAH-dur-ing) joining pieces of metal by putting a small amount of heated, melted metal between them

terminals (TUR-muh-nuhlz) Y-shaped metal parts that are attached to the end of a wire to increase the contact surface area

volts (VOLTZ) units for measuring the force of an electrical current or the stored power of a battery

Find Out More

BOOKS

Lockwood, Sophie. *Super Cool Science Experiments: Electricity*. Ann Arbor, MI: Cherry Lake Publishing, 2010.

O'Neill, Terence, and Josh Williams. *Arduino*. Ann Arbor, MI: Cherry Lake Publishing, 2013.

Toth-Chernin, Jan. *E-Textiles*. Ann Arbor, MI: Cherry Lake Publishing, 2013.

WEB SITES

DIY
www.diy.org
Earn badges by completing all sorts of maker projects, from making circuits to beekeeping!

Squishy Circuits—University of St. Thomas
www.stthomas.edu/squishycircuits
Make Squishy Circuits dough, learn techniques for making circuits, and find out where you can order components.

Sylvia's Super-Awesome Maker Show!
www.sylviashow.com
Tune in to this Web series to learn how to make Squishy Circuits and many other maker projects.

Index

About the Authors

Kristin Fontichiaro (left) teaches at the University of Michigan School of Information, where she coordinates the Michigan Makers makerspaces for kids. AnnMarie P. Thomas (right) is an associate professor of engineering at the University of St. Thomas in St. Paul, Minnesota, a maker, and a mom to two daughters.